EXTRAORDINARY ANIMALS

DANGEROUS ANIMALS

Andrew Brown

CRABTREE
Publishing Company

CRABTREE
Publishing Company

350 Fifth Avenue
Suite 3308
New York, NY 10118

360 York Road, R.R.4
Niagara-on-the-Lake
Ontario L0S 1J0

73 Lime Walk
Headington, Oxford
England OX3 7AD

Editor **Bobbie Kalman**
Assistant Editor **Petrina Gentile**
Designer **Melissa Stokes**

Illustrations by

Front cover: Wildlife Art Agency (main), Wayne Ford/WLAA, Elisabeth Smith, Valérie Stetten; Back cover: John Cox
Robin Boutell/WLAA (p. 18–19, 26–29), John Cox (p. 24–25), Barry Croucher/WLAA (p. 13), Wayne Ford/WLAA (p. 20–21),
Steve Kingston (p. 22–23), Gary Martin/WLAA (p. 8), John Morris/WLAA (p. 7), Elisabeth Smith (p. 6–7, 16–17, 24),
Valérie Stetten (p. 10–11, 12–13, 30–31), Kim Thompson (p. 14–15), Wildlife Art Agency (p. 8–9)

Created by
Marshall Cavendish Books, London
(a division of Marshall Cavendish Partworks Ltd.)
119 Wardour Street, London, W1V 3TD, England

First printed 1997
Copyright © 1997 Marshall Cavendish Ltd.

Cataloging-in-Publication Data

Brown, Andrew, 1972-
Dangerous animals
(Extraordinary animals series)
Includes index.
ISBN 0-86505-560-2 (bound)   ISBN 0-86505-568-8 (pbk.)
1. Dangerous animals – Juvenile literature.
I. Title.   II. Series: Brown, Andrew, 1972-   .   Extraordinary animals series.
QL100.B76 1997   j591   LC 96-46982

Printed and bound in Malaysia

CONTENTS

INTRODUCTION

Many animals are strong and vicious fighters. Some attack and kill animals for food. Others fight to protect themselves or defend their territory. Some animals have big, powerful paws or tusks. Others have deadly bites that can kill an animal in seconds!

SHARKS

are dangerous animals. Many will kill and eat almost anything in the water.

THE WOLVERINE

is very strong. Its powerful body, teeth, and claws help it attack animals that are larger than itself.

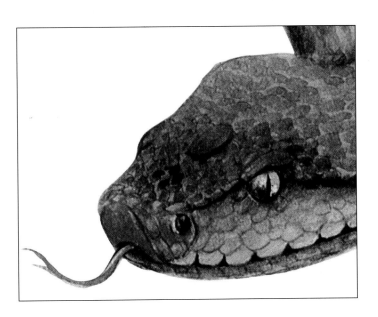

SOME SNAKES

have fangs filled with deadly poison. One bite could kill an adult elephant!

TIGERS

have large, sharp teeth, called canines. The teeth help the tiger hold onto prey.

LIONS

The lion is a powerful and frightening animal. It is often called the King of the Beasts.

A lion's family is called a pride. A female lion is called a lioness. She is usually the hunter of the pride.

Zebras and wildebeests are the lion's favorite foods. The lioness hides behind grass and sneaks up on its prey. When the time is right, she attacks. She may jump on the animal's back and knock it to the ground. Then the lioness sinks her deadly teeth into the animal's throat, killing it instantly.

▼▼▼ **THE MANE**

is the fur around the lion's neck. It makes the male lion look large and frightening. It also protects the lion's throat when it fights.

THE LANGUAGE OF LIONS

Lions have many ways of communicating with one another. They have different growls, meows, moans, grunts, and hisses. (1) The lion's call can range from a gentle meow to a frightening, deep-throated roar! Cubs make soft, purring sounds when they are happy. Female lions snarl at cubs when they are misbehaving.

Lions often use their bodies to communicate. To show affection, they wave their tails and touch each other. They also make faces. (2) Male lions show their teeth when they are scared or about to attack an enemy. (3) They wrinkle up their nose when they smell the tracks of another lion.

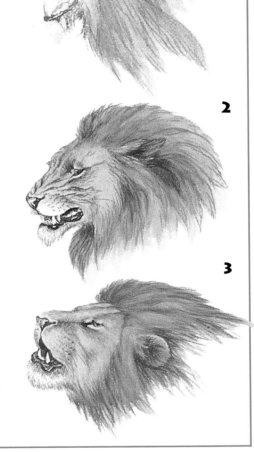

1

2

3

◀◀◀ **THE FRONT LEGS** have strong, powerful muscles. The lion uses them to attack large animals.

◀◀◀ **THE BACK LEGS** give the lion extra running and jumping power when it is chasing prey.

TIGERS

The tiger is the largest type of big cat. It can kill an animal twice its size!

The tiger hunts alone in the evening. It moves silently, listening for prey. The tiger attacks by jumping on its prey's back and biting its neck. Once the animal is dead, the tiger drags it away and eats it.

Tigers need a lot of food. They can eat 100 lb (45 kg) of meat in one meal—that is the same as eating 40 hamburgers at once! Tigers do not normally hurt people, but if they feel threatened, they may attack.

THE TIGER'S TEETH

The tiger has sharp front teeth, called canines. Some canines are five inches (13 cm) long. The canines help the tiger hold onto prey. The smaller teeth inside the tiger's mouth are used to cut up tough flesh. The tiger needs its teeth to survive. Without them, the tiger would not be able to hunt, and soon it would starve to death.

▼▼▼ THE TIGER

has a striped coat. When it hides in long grass, the tiger is almost invisible.

▼▼▼ THE PREY

is attacked from behind. The tiger bites into the prey's neck and chokes it to death.

SNAKES

There are many types of snakes. Some snakes are called "constrictors." They have very strong muscles. They wrap themselves around their prey and squeeze them to death.

Other snakes have sharp, hollow teeth, called fangs. When these snakes bite into their prey, they inject deadly poison.

Snakes usually eat small birds and animals such as rats, frogs, and other snakes. Some even eat big animals such as deer. Snakes do not chew their prey—they swallow it whole!

▲▲▲ THE TEETH are small. The hollow poison fangs are large. The snake uses its teeth to hold onto prey.

DEADLY POISON

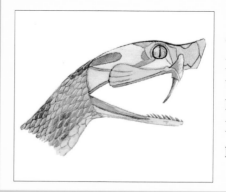

Some snakes have fangs filled with deadly poison. Just a tiny bit of poison, or venom, is strong enough to kill 500 people! Many people have died from snake bites. In India, snakes kill about 20,000 people each year!

▼▼▼ THE BODY

of the snake is very flexible.
It expands easily so that the
snake can swallow and eat
very large prey.

▼▼▼ THE SKIN

is dry, even though it looks
wet. The snake sheds its skin
several times a year. It then
grows a new skin.

EAGLES

Some birds hunt prey. The largest and most powerful bird of prey is the eagle.

The eagle has excellent eyesight. When it searches for food, the eagle soars high in the sky, so it can spot animals far away. Sometimes it can see animals over a mile (3 km) away.

Once an eagle spots an animal, it swoops down and grabs the prey. It can fly up to 100 miles an hour (160 km/h)!

The eagle uses its long, sharp claws, called talons, to grab and kill its prey. It carries the prey back to its nest and tears it into small pieces. The eagle feeds the pieces to its chicks and then eats the rest.

THE BEAK ▲▲▲
is sharp and hooked. The eagle uses its beak to tear prey into pieces.

▲▲▲ **THE WINGS**
are wide and powerful.
They help the eagle soar
in the sky.

◀◀◀ **THE LEGS**
are large and thick. They have
sharp talons that help the bird
grab and crush its prey.

THE EAGLE'S DIET

Most eagles catch small animals, such as
rabbits, chickens, snakes, and foxes. Some
feed on larger prey, such as sheep, deer,
antelopes, and jackals.

The North American bald eagle hunts
fish. It uses its talons to pluck fish right
out of the water! Sometimes it will go
completely underwater.

JACKALS

The jackal is a type of wild dog that lives in Africa and Asia. It is a scavenger, which means it eats the food that other animals have killed.

The jackal also hunts small creatures, such as birds and mice. It sneaks up and pounces on its prey. Sometimes jackals hunt in groups. They attack large prey, such as antelopes and zebras. Several jackals may distract a female gazelle, while another attacks her baby.

All the jackals in the group share the food. Each one takes a piece of meat and runs away to eat it. If it cannot eat it all at once, the jackal hides the rest for later.

▶ ▶ ▶ **VULTURES**
often try to steal other animals' prey, but the jackals below will protect their food.

▼ ▼ ▼ **A ZEBRA**
will provide enough meat to feed two or three jackals for days.

WOLVES

are large and pointed. The wolf has excellent hearing. It can detect faint noises miles away.

Wolves are strong hunters. They can kill almost any type of animal including horses, moose, and caribou.

Wolves work in teams, called packs, when they are hunting animals in herds. The pack surrounds the herd and attacks the weakest animal.

Wolves are affectionate with other members of their pack, but if a wolf from another pack comes too close, it will be attacked.

THE WOLF'S MOUTH

When the wolf threatens other animals, it snarls and shows its ferocious teeth *(right)*. If it is frightened, the wolf closes its lips to hide its teeth. When a wolf loses a fight with another animal, it sticks out its tongue!

▼▼▼ THE BODY

is powerful and slim. It is built
to run for long distances.

▼▼▼ THE FUR

is soft and thick. It keeps
the wolf warm and dry.
The color of wolves' fur
ranges from light to dark.

◄◄◄ THE LEGS

are long and strong. The
front feet have five toes.
The back feet have four.

WOLVERINES

The wolverine lives alone in the remote forests of Canada, Alaska, Asia, and northern Europe.

In the summer, the wolverine eats mice, rats, and small birds. In the winter, it hunts larger prey, such as mountain goats and reindeer. It can even kill an adult caribou that is ten times its weight!

The wolverine is not a fast runner. Since it cannot chase its prey, the wolverine hides behind rocks or in trees and pounces on the animal's back. It holds onto its prey tightly. When the animal falls down, the wolverine tears its catch apart with its sharp teeth. It eats what it can and hides the rest for later.

Few predators dare to attack a wolverine. They know the animal is ferocious. Besides humans, who kill wolverines for their fur, packs of wolves are the only real threat. They can rip a wolverine to shreds in seconds!

▼▼▼ THE TEETH

of the wolverine are so strong
that they can crush bone and
bite through flesh in seconds.

WILD BOARS

The male wild boar is a very fierce animal. It has razor-sharp teeth and tusks. The male boar uses its tusks when it fights other male boars.

If a boar is threatened by another animal or person, it will usually run away. Sometimes the boar will charge its attacker.

THE BOAR'S TEETH AND TUSKS

The wild boar has some very dangerous weapons. It has two sharp tusks on its lower jaw. The tusks are actually long, hollow teeth. They grow from the side of the jaw. As the tusks grow outside the boar's mouth, they curve backwards toward the eyes.

The other teeth are also very sharp. A wild boar's bite is thought to be worse than a lion's bite!

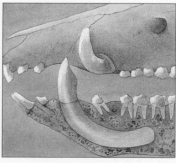

▼▼▼ THE SKIN

is very thick. The coat has lots
of hard bristles that protect the
animal when it fights.

▼▼▼ THE BODY

has tough muscles and
bones. Some boars
weigh twice as much as
a grown man.

THE LEGS ▶▶▶

are short, but the wild
boar can still run very fast.

GRIZZLY BEARS

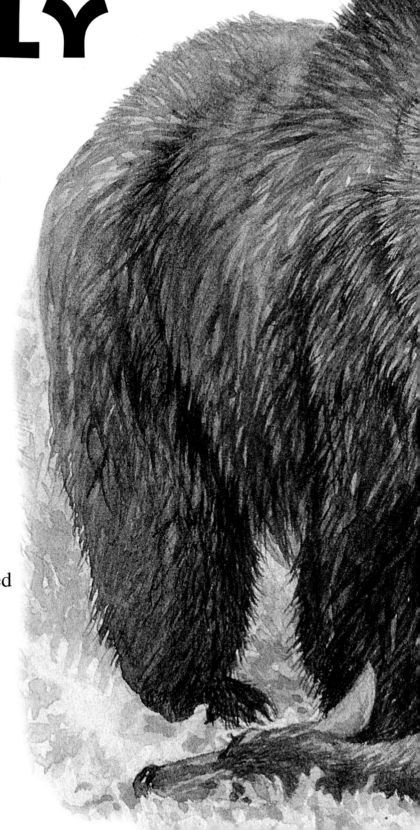

The grizzly bear lives in Canada and the United States. It is the most aggressive bear. It kills and eats many animals— even its own cubs!

Grizzly bears have very powerful front paws. Each paw has five long, sharp claws. A bear can kill an animal as big as a moose with just one swipe of its paw. When it attacks, the grizzly shows its terrifying teeth.

Grizzly bears are usually not dangerous to humans, but if they become frightened or angry, they may attack.

The grizzly bear is large. When it stands on its back legs, it is taller than a grown man. Grizzlies can grow to almost ten feet (3 m) tall and weigh 900 lb (400 kg)!

◄◄◄ PREY

is often dragged away and hidden in a favorite spot. The grizzly covers it with dirt and leaves and eats it later.

HIPPOS

Hippos spend most of the day wallowing in water. Male hippos can get angry very easily. When they do, they are dangerous. Male hippos often start fights and hit each other with their teeth to see who is the strongest. Sometimes they get hurt or even killed.

Hippos are also dangerous to people. In Africa, hippos kill more people than any other animal. If a boat comes too close, they will knock it over, drowning the people inside. Sometimes they also charge at people and crush them with their weight.

SAVAGE JAWS

When a hippo wants to scare an enemy, it opens its jaws and shows its enormous front teeth. This is called jawing. Some teeth can grow up to 20 inches (50 cm) long! The hippo uses them to defend itself and attack enemies.

learn how to fight when they
are about seven years old.
One male will fight to be the
head of the group, usually
when it is 20 years old.

ORCAS

Orcas, also known as killer whales, are the most powerful hunters in the sea. They kill and eat almost anything that lives in the water.

The orca uses sound to find prey. It makes clicking noises that travel through the water. When they hit an object, they bounce back to the killer whale. When the whale hears the clicks, it can easily find the location of the prey.

THE JAWS ▶▶▶
are big and powerful. They can open so wide that small seals can be swallowed whole.

resting on the shore are not safe from whale attacks. The orca swims onto shore to grab its prey.

Orcas usually hunt together in large groups. Big fish, such as salmon, are the orca's favorite food.

When they have found a school of fish, the whales surround it. Then they force the fish toward the seashore, where it is difficult to escape (*see below*). One by one, the whales swim toward the fish and gulp down as many as they can.

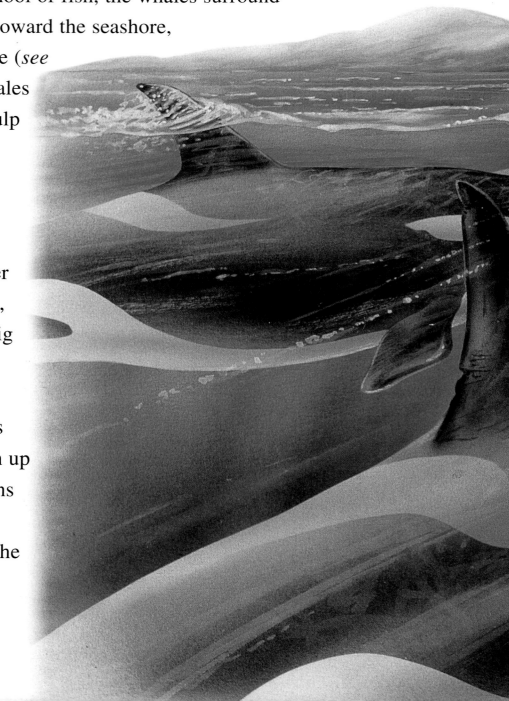

Orcas also hunt bigger animals such as penguins, dolphins, walruses, and other whales. Each orca has sharp, pointed teeth that can tear big chunks out of its victims.

In frozen waters, some orcas swim under the ice and push up against it. If seals or penguins are resting on top of the ice, they will slide straight into the mouths of the orcas nearby.

SHARKS

Sharks are one of the most dangerous sea animals. They spend all their time swimming, hunting, and eating prey.

Sharks use their excellent sense of smell and sound to find prey. They usually eat fish, seals, turtles, and other sharks. When they attack, sharks swim toward their prey with their mouth open and gulp up everything in their way. Some sharks have even been found with car parts inside their stomachs!

Most large sharks will attack people. They can injure or kill easily. Except tiger sharks, most sharks rarely eat humans.

THE NOSE ▲▲▲
is very sensitive. Sharks can smell a single drop of blood in the water miles away.

▲▲▲ **THE JAWS**
are very powerful. They are 15 times stronger than human jaws.

THE SHARK'S TEETH

The shark's teeth are shaped like triangles. They can grow as large as the palm of a child's hand. The shark's teeth and powerful jaws help it bite through even the strongest of turtle shells.

Most sharks usually have about 3,000 teeth. They are always growing new teeth. When they lose a tooth, a new one appears from underneath. During its lifetime, a shark will have had more than 20,000 teeth!

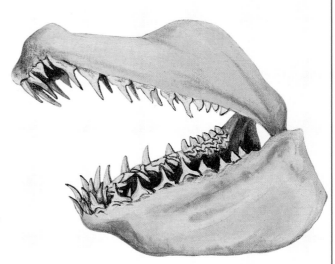

▼▼▼ THE SKIN

of a shark is very rough. Before the invention of sandpaper, shark skin was used to polish wood.

INDEX

GLOSSARY

antelope – an animal that is related to the goat and has short horns

caribou – a type of large deer that has a heavy coat and large antlers

flexible – something that is able to bend without breaking

gazelle – a type of antelope that has a yellowish-brown coat and curved horns

moose – the largest member of the deer family

prey – an animal that is hunted by another animal for food

sandpaper – a strong, heavy paper coated with sand

wildebeest – a type of antelope with a long tail and short horns that curve upwards